SPEED MACHINES

JETS

BY MATT SCHEFF

SportsZone

An Imprint of Abdo Publishing
www.abdopublishing.com

www.abdopublishing.com

Published by Abdo Publishing, a division of ABDO, PO Box 398166,
Minneapolis, Minnesota 55439. Copyright © 2015 by Abdo Consulting Group,
Inc. International copyrights reserved in all countries. No part of this
book may be reproduced in any form without written permission from the
publisher. SportsZone™ is a trademark and logo of Abdo Publishing.

Printed in the United States of America, North Mankato, Minnesota
082014
012015

Cover Photo: iStockphoto
Interior Photos: iStockphoto, 1; Sitthixay Ditthavong/AP Images, 4-5; Nam Y.
Huh/AP Images, 6-7; John T. Daniels/AP Images, 8-9; AP Images, 9, 24; Ho/
Heinkel/AP Images, 10-11; Robert E. Klein/AP Images, 12-13; Heiko Junge/epa/
Corbis, 14-15; Hassan Ammar/AP Images, 16-17; Felipe Dana/AP Images, 18-19;
Mindaugas Kulbis/AP Images, 20-21; Erik Tham/Corbis, 20; Domenico Stinellis/AP
Images, 22-23, 31; Geert Vanden Wijngaert/AP Images, 24-25; Daniel Reinhardt/
picture-alliance/dpa/AP Images, 26-27; Ted S. Warren/AP Images, 28-29

Editor: Chrös McDougall
Series Designer: Nikki Farinella

Library of Congress Control Number: 2014944189

Cataloging-in-Publication Data
Scheff, Matt.
 Jets / Matt Scheff.
   p. cm. -- (Speed machines)
ISBN 978-1-62403-612-5 (lib. bdg.)
Includes bibliographical references and index.
1. Jet planes--Juvenile literature.   I. Title.
629.133--dc23
                                                    2014944189

CONTENTS

Blue Angels fly overhead at the
Chicago Air and Water Show.

SHOWTIME

Hundreds of thousands of people line up along Lake Michigan in Chicago, Illinois. They're all there for the Chicago Air and Water Show. It is the biggest free show of its kind in the United States. Everyone looks up as the roar of six F/A-18 Hornet jet airplanes fills the air. It's the US Navy's Blue Angels, the highlight of the show!

The Blue Angels are known for their daring stunts.

FAST FACT

During a maneuver called the Diamond 360, Blue Angel jets fly just 18 inches (46 cm) apart from each other!

The bright blue-and-yellow planes streak overhead. Four of the planes fly in a tight diamond formation. They're so close that their wings almost touch! The other two planes streak in from opposite directions. They whiz by each other in a thrilling high-speed pass. The crowd cheers at the daring stunts. And the show has only just begun.

THE HISTORY OF JET AIRPLANES

People have long been fascinated with flight. Brothers Wilbur and Orville Wright built the first successful airplane in 1903. The earliest airplanes were powered by spinning propellers. But these airplanes were limited in how high and how fast they could go. By the 1930s, inventors were working on a new, faster engine called a jet engine.

The Wright brothers test out their first airplane in 1903.

Most early airplanes were powered by propellers.

The first modern jet engine, or turbojet, flew in Germany in 1939. The Heinkel He 178 prototype's jet engines worked by pulling in air, heating it, and shooting it out at high speeds. This new type of aircraft could fly faster and higher than propeller-driven aircraft. Any aircraft powered by one or more jet engines is a known as a jet.

The Heinkel He 178 shown in 1939.

FAST FACT

The first jetliners to fly from England to South Africa needed 21 hours and five stops. Today that flight can be made in 11 hours with no stops.

Jet airplanes went on to rule the sky. Air forces around the world built jet fighters and bombers. In 1952, the first commercial jetliner carried passengers from London, England, to Johannesburg, South Africa. The first jetliners were a marvel. But early models suffered several terrible crashes. Engineers continued to improve the design. Within a decade, jet travel was quite common and much safer.

The Concorde was the world's fastest passenger jet.

The Concorde passenger jet could travel as fast as 1,354 miles per hour (2,179 km/h). That is more than twice the speed of sound!

PARTS OF A JET AIRPLANE

Jets come in all kinds of shapes and sizes, from military fighters to commercial jetliners. But they all share a few common features. The main body of the aircraft is called the fuselage. The cockpit lies within the fuselage. The pilot controls the plane from the cockpit.

FAST FACT

The Antonov An-225 is the world's biggest jet. It's almost as long as a football field and can weigh more than 1 million pounds (453,592 kg).

The Antonov An-225 comes in to land at an airport in Norway.

Wings stick out from the fuselage. Jet wings, also called airfoils, have a special curved shape. This shape forces air that moves over the wings to go faster than the air that travels under them. Slower air has higher pressure than fast-moving air. So the air under the wings pushes up on them, giving the jet lift.

A US Air Force F-18 fighter jet takes off from an aircraft carrier.

Flaps attached to each wing allow the pilot to climb or descend. To turn, a pilot controls hinged panels called ailerons as well as a rudder on the tail of the plane.

Jets need landing gear to touch down safely. This system of wheels tucks up into the fuselage during flight.

An F-18 jet lands on
an aircraft carrier.

Powerful jet engines give airplanes thrust.

The jet turbine engine is the heart of a jet airplane.
The front of the jet engine allows air into an intake.
This air flows into the combustion chamber. There,
fuel burns and rapidly heats the air. The hot air
expands. It is forced through spinning blades called
turbines and out the back of the engine. This gives the
jet its thrust.

An F-15 Eagle cruises through the sky.

FAST FACT

The fastest jet in the world is the X-43A. This remote-controlled aircraft can travel 10 times faster than the speed of sound!

PHOTO DIAGRAM

1. Cockpit
2. Fuselage
3. Wing
4. Rudder
5. Landing Gear
6. Jet Engine

22

The B-2 Spirit stealth bomber
is undetectable by radar.

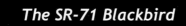

The SR-71 Blackbird

FAST FACT

The SR-71 Blackbird is the highest-flying jet. It once reached 85,069 feet (25,929 m) above sea level. That's more than 16 miles (25.7 km)!

JETS IN ACTION

Jets have all kinds of uses. Air forces around the world use heavy cargo jets and bombers. Quick and powerful fighter jets are loaded with weapons. Spy planes are built to avoid detection. Some spy planes do this by flying through the upper reaches of Earth's atmosphere. Other jets have stealth technology. The B-2 bomber has a complex shape that makes it invisible to radar.

Jet airplanes designed to carry passengers are called airliners. Huge airliners such as the Boeing 747 can carry approximately 500 passengers. They can fly 8,000 miles (12,875 km) or more without refueling.

FAST FACT

The world's largest airliner is the A380 Superjumbo. It can carry more than 800 passengers.

The Boeing 747 is one of the biggest passenger planes.

Some small jets are made for racing. Pilots can fly them in events such as the National Championship Air Races in Reno, Nevada. Pilots roar around a set course at more than 500 miles per hour (805 km/h). Their ultra-fast jets perform high-speed turns and battle for position and clean air in a race to the finish line.

The Patriots Jet Team performs at an air show.

GLOSSARY

aileron
A hinged panel on an airplane wing that allows the pilot to control the plane's roll, which affects its direction.

clean air
Air that has not been touched by another airplane.

combustion chamber
The part of a jet engine where fuel is burned to heat up the air inside.

flaps
Parts of a wing that can be raised or lowered to control the plane's upward or downward motion.

formation
An arrangement of airplanes flying together.

fuselage
The main body of an airplane that holds passengers and cargo.

intake
The opening at the front of a jet engine that allows air to enter.

landing gear
An airplane's wheels.

propeller
A set of rapidly spinning blades that propel some aircraft.

rudder
A hinged panel on the tail of an airplane that helps a pilot control the plane's direction.

stealth
Undetectable to radar.

thrust
Forward force produced by a jet engine.

turbine
A set of rapidly spinning blades inside a jet engine. The turbine produces energy as air rushes through.

FOR MORE INFORMATION

Books

Morey, Allan. *Fighter Jets*. Minneapolis, MN: Jump!, 2014.

Petrie, Kristin. *Airplanes*. Edina, MN: Abdo Publishing Co., 2008.

Tieck, Sarah. *Jets*. Edina, MN: Abdo Publishing Co., 2010.

Websites

To learn more about Speed Machines, visit booklinks.abdopublishing.com. These links are routinely monitored and updated to provide the most current information available.

INDEX

ABOUT THE AUTHOR

[...] Schell is a freelance author and lifelong motor sports [...] living in Minnesota.